Be Fille

"God is love. The pers(
and God lives in him or

"God's love has been
Holy Spirit" Romans 5:ᴗ.

God is a personal spirit of infinite energy, and this mighty energy is love. The very essence and life-force of God is love.

Right now this very God who created the universe, is right there with you, and He desires to embrace you in love and to pour His love into your heart.

Lord Jesus, I repent of all selfishness and bitterness, and I desire to be permeated to the very depths of my being by Your Love.

Thank You, O Holy Spirit, that You are pouring your love into my heart.

May my heart be so filled with Your love, that it will begin to shine out through my eyes.

(Pause. Allow yourself to be embraced by love.)

1

Create Heaven On Earth

"The person who truly loves has been reborn of God and knows God" 1 John 4:7.

"My dear people, we are already the children of God and when He appears we shall be like Him" 1 John 3:2.

God is love. Everyone in Heaven has been transformed by love and radiates love.

The challenge for us is to create a little bit of Heaven on earth, starting in our own homes, and then reaching out to wherever we go.

We can only do that by creating an atmosphere of love, acceptance, encouragement and understanding.

Lord, for this day, may I be able to create a little bit of Heaven on earth, starting in my own home.

May I greet every person with love in my eyes.

May I bring real blessing into the life of some person this very day.

(Pause. Ask the Holy Spirit to give you a mental picture of yourself creating a little bit of Heaven on earth.)

When Under Attack

"Blessed are the peacemakers. They are God's own sons and daughters" Mt 5:9.

"Love your enemies and bless those who torment you. Then you will be children of your Father who causes His sun to shine on bad men and good alike" Mt 5:44.

Because God is love, being His true child involves learning to love one's enemies.

If you have to live in a situation where the home or the workplace is 'hell on earth', cry your pain out to God.

Then pray, that with God's help, you will still be able to have love in your heart.

Lord, You prayed, "Father, forgive them for they know not what they do." Help me to make that prayer my own.

I bring to You all the pain and upset I now experience.

Thank You, that with your help, I am going to be able to cope, and to still be a loving person.

(Pause. Become aware of Jesus giving you strength)

A Heart Transplant

"I shall cleanse you to the depth of your being. I shall give you a new heart, and impart my Spirit to you. I shall remove your heart of stone, and give you a heart full of love. " Ezek 36:25-27

Love and selfishness do not mix. Neither do love and bitterness, or love and meanness, or love and lust, or love and greed, mix.

God loves you, but before you can grow in His love and experience ongoing inner healing, your heart needs to be cleansed.

Lord Jesus, I long for this new heart; to have a heart filled with love.

Deliver me, Lord, from all hardness of heart.
Deliver me, Lord, from all selfishness of heart.
Deliver me, Lord, from all meanness of heart.
Deliver me, Lord, from all bitterness of heart.
Deliver me, Lord, from all impurity of heart.

Heal and cleanse my heart, Lord Jesus.
Make it a fitting home for You to live in.

(Pause. Mentally picture Jesus filling your heart with love.)

To Be Born Again

"Unless one is born again of water and the Holy Spirit one cannot be part of the Lord's kingdom." John 3:5

Nicodemus was a man of prayer. He was totally dedicated. Yet Jesus told him that he needed to be born again.

Up to then, his religion had come from his own efforts. "What is born of the flesh is flesh" John 3:6.

Instead He needed to have God come alive in His heart and to be transformed from within by Love. "What is born of the Spirit is spirit."

Lord Jesus, I desire the fullness of the rebirth. Come alive in my heart and flood me with Your love.

O Holy Spirit penetrate every area of my being with Your healing, cleansing and delivering power.

Thank You, Jesus, that You have won for me the right to total inner transformation, including the complete healing and cleansing of my heart, my mind my emotions, my attitudes, and my sexuality.

(Pause. Become conscious of Jesus within you.)

A Sacrament of Healing

"Confess your sins to one another and pray with one another that you may be healed" James 4:16.

If you desire Confession to become a sacrament of ongoing healing, then find a regular confessor to whom you can be totally honest, and go to Confession face to face.

Since I took those steps, the Sacrament of Confession has become a source of ongoing miracles for me. It can be the same for you.

Lord Jesus, I come to You in sincere repentance for every sin I have ever committed. But I also come with total trust in Your mercy, accepting You as my Lord and Saviour.

Lord, bless every person into whose life I have ever brought hurt or disappointment, (especially ....)

And grant me the grace to be totally honest with myself, with You and with my confessor.

(Pause. Examine your conscience.)

Surrendering One's Ambitions

"Unless you change and become like little children, you will not be part of my kingdom. The one who humbles himself like a little child is the greatest in the kingdom of heaven." Mt. 18:3-4

In the early stages of the spiritual life, it is normal to have the ambition to achieve, the ambition to be recognised, and the ambition to be a success in human terms.

But if we are to be the living presence of Jesus in the world, all these ambitions need to be surrendered to Jesus.

Lord Jesus, I renounce all self-seeking ambition, and all divisive ambition.
I renounce the desire to be recognised as important, and the desire to be seen to be influential.
Lord, I entrust all my ambitions to You.

My one ambition now is to become
Your voice, Your hands, Your face;
To live in total union with You;
And to help my loved ones to do the same.

(Pause. Desire total union with Jesus.)

To Pray With Voice of Jesus

Before appointing the twelve, "Jesus went up into the hills and spent the entire night in prayer" Luke 9:29.

Before Jesus cried over Jerusalem, you can be sure that He prayed long and hard for its conversion. Prayer wins opportunities for people, but they can still reject those opportunities.

Yet Jesus saw mighty answers to prayer, and so too can we - if we learn to live in Him, and to pray with His voice.

Lord Jesus,
May my thoughts spring from Your thoughts;
May my prayers spring from Your prayers;
May it no longer be I who pray,
But You Lord, who prays through me.

May my heart be united with Your heart;
May my faith be energised by Your faith;
And may I see powerful answers to prayer.

(Pause. Invite Jesus to pray through you.)

Seeing Prayers Answered

"If you live in Me, and my words live in you, then you may ask for whatever you wish and you will have it" John 15:6.

There are three necessary steps for regular answer to prayer.

1. Invite Jesus to live in you.

2. Then learn to live in Him. For this to happen, you need to be delivered from your compulsions and to be transformed by love.

3. Have His words come alive in you. Those who read the Bible have a major advantage here.

Lord Jesus I do desire to live in deep union with You, and for your words to come alive within me.

Give me a love for the Bible, and show me how to read it.

With this desire in my heart, I now bring to You my special intention ....

Thank You, Jesus, that you are answering my prayer.

(Mentally picture Jesus embracing your intention.)

Renounce Judgementalism

"Do not judge and you will not be judged" Luke 6:37.

"Why do you see the speck in your brother's eye and do not see the beam in your own eye?" Mt. 7:3.

To have the mind of Jesus and to pray with His voice, one must renounce judgementalism and all unloving thoughts and seek to be delivered from them.

Judgementalism is often a symptom that there is anger and insecurity in one's own heart that needs to be dealt with.

**Deliver me, Lord, from the spirit of judgementalism.
Deliver me, Lord, from all inner anger and insecurity.**

Become aware of that part of your inner being from where the judgementalism or anger arises. Place your hand to it and pray,

Lord Jesus, permeate this part of my inner self with your healing love.

Pause. Become aware of your inner self being permeated by LOVE for a moment. Then add,

**Thank You, Jesus, that You will enable me to see other people through Your eyes,
And to love them with Your love for them.**

10

Called To Become Jesus

"He or she who eats my flesh and drinks my blood lives in Me and I live in him or her." John 6:56

"We are to become the Body of Christ, His own flesh and blood." Pope Benedict (WYD 2005)

The first step is to have Jesus come alive in one's heart. But Jesus calls us to something far more radical:- to live in Him.

Our calling is nothing less than to become the living presence of Jesus in the world - to become His hands, His feet, His voice, His face, His heart, and His mind.

But to have "the mind of Christ", (1 Cor 2:16), we need "a complete make-over of our minds." Rom 12:2

Lord Jesus, transform my mind by the healing, cleansing and delivering power of the Holy Spirit.

Lord, help me to spot and to renounce every thought that does not come from You.

Lord Jesus, teach me how to become Your mind, Your hands, Your feet, Your eyes, Your ears, Your face, and Your voice in today's world.

(Pause. Invite the Holy Spirit to transform your mind.)

One's Suffering

"In my flesh, I complete what is lacking in Christ's afflictions for the sake of His body, that is the Church" Col 1:24.

When we live in Jesus and He in us, our entire being, including our sufferings become united with Jesus living within us.

Our sufferings, including tiredness and inner anguish, then become an extension of His redemptive suffering.

It is, however, the risen Jesus who lives within us, so even as we offer up our sufferings in union with His sufferings, we pray also to be touched by the power of His resurrection.

Lord Jesus, I surrender myself and all my sufferings to You who are living within me.

Sanctify my sufferings, Lord Jesus. May blessing be released through them, (especially for ....)

But I also pray, Lord, to be touched by the power of Your resurrection:- to be lifted up, to be given strength, and to experience your healing love.

(Become conscious of Jesus within you. Then surrender your sufferings to Him, and draw strength from Him.)

Being The Hands Of Jesus

"Since you were faithful in small things, I will put you in charge of large matters." Luke 19:17

Jesus spent some thirty years doing the ordinary things.

We are called to be the hands of Jesus and the feet of Jesus in everything we do - even when washing dishes or sweeping the floor.

Often we desire to do something big or exciting immediately, but normally we must first mature while being faithful in little things.

Lord, help me to realise that in my daily work, my hands can be Your hands and my feet Your feet.

May I do my daily work in deep union with You, Lord, and under Your anointing. May I make all the right choices, and take all things in my stride.

Grant me a special appreciation for those who spend their lives doing the more menial tasks. To them, Lord, may I be Your face, Your ears and Your voice.

(Pause. Look at your hands. Desire to use them as the hands of Jesus in your daily work.)

"Tell Your Family"

Jesus told the man who had been delivered, "Return to your home and tell your family how much God has done for you." Luke 8:39

If you love Jesus, you will thirst for the day when each member of your family has a living relationship with Him.

You will have a vision of Jesus being Lord of your home.

And you will long for Him to be Lord of the homes of your children and your children's children.

Lord Jesus, I invite You to consecrate my home and family to Your Sacred Heart.

May each member of my family come to a living relationship with You and establish You as Lord of their homes.

**I ask especially for .... & .... &...........
Immerse them in the rays of your mercy.**

Lord, teach me how to become Your living presence to my family.

(Mentally picture Jesus blessing key family members.)

The Eucharist

"This is My body which will be given up for you. ... This is My blood which will be offered for you ... Do this is memory of Me." (See Lk 22:20)

Do you realise that in Mass we are called to offer our own lives in union with Jesus to the eternal Father?

Only then do we fulfil the command, "Do this in memory of Me."

**Lord Jesus, in each Mass,
Help me to offer my body along with Your body;
To offer my blood along with Your blood;
To offer my life along with Your life.**

(Pause and unite yourself with Jesus' self-offering to the Father.)

Lord Jesus, as I unite myself with You each time in Mass, I pray that your blessings will be poured out upon ... (Write your intentions here)

....

....

Television and Papers

"Don't let the world determine how you think, but let God be the one who moulds your thinking" Rom 12:1.

"If your eye causes you to sin, pluck it out." Mk 9:47

Television can be a wonderful gift, but it can also be a source of great corruption. The same is true of both the internet and newspapers.

Invite Jesus to become Lord of your TV, your computers and of what you read.

Lord Jesus, I consecrate my television, my computer and my newspapers to you.

Lord, I pray for the grace to only watch and read what You and I, Lord, can watch and read together.

Grant my family the grace, Lord, to reject all the works of the evil one in the media.

(Especially protect .... from all evil in ....).

I also pray, Lord, for the raising up of dynamic Christian television and radio in our country.

(Pause. Hold this prayer in your heart before Jesus)

Heroic Love

"Father, as You are in Me, and I am in You, may they so live in us, that the world will recognise that it was You who sent me." John 17:21

If your heart is to be united with the heart of Jesus, then it needs to learn to love with the love of Jesus.

This isn't possible in human terms, but it is possible by the power of the Holy Spirit. Think of someone you find it hard to love. Become conscious of Jesus' love for him (her). Then unite yourself with His love for him (her).

Lord Jesus, help me to surrender all my hurts and all my anger to You, and to become united with You in Your love for even the worst sinners.

Whatever mistakes people have made, whatever problems they now have, whatever hurt they have caused, grant me the grace to still love them.

Grant me the grace, Lord, to become the living embodiment of Your love, especially to my family.

(Pause. Become aware of the infinite love of Jesus who is within you. Invite it to flow through your very veins.)

17

Jesus, I Trust In You

"Commit your cause to the Lord, trust in Him and he will act on your behalf." Ps. 37:5

Jesus told St. Faustina,
"The graces of my mercy are drawn by means of one vessel only, and that is - trust.

"The more a soul trusts, the more it will receive.

"Souls that trust boundlessly are a great comfort to me, because I pour all the treasures of my graces into them."
Diary 1578

Deliver me, Lord, from the spirit of worry.
Deliver me, Lord, from the spirit of mental agitation.
Deliver me, Lord, from the spirit of fear.
Deliver me, Lord, from the spirit of anxiety.

Lord Jesus, I entrust every situation to You, especially ....

Lord, for the grace to really trust You,
The grace to trust that Your way is always best,
The grace to know that You will never let me down.

(Pause. Entrust your whole life to Jesus)

18

To Be Guided By You, Lord

"The Lord desires to guide you always and He will satisfy your desire for what is right." Isaiah 58:11

"The Lord leads the humble into His plan for their lives." Ps. 25:9

We are not pure spirits. We will never be able to perfectly hear God in every situation, so prayer for guidance needs to be approached with real humility.

Yet, if we seek His guidance with humility and trust, then Jesus will guide us.

Lord Jesus, I do desire to hear your voice. I do desire to be guided by You in all things.

Lord, if I am ever stepping outside Your plan for my life, block me. Put obstacles in my path.

Likewise if I am slow in responding to Your call, do something to stir me up, Lord.

O Holy Spirit, make me sensitive to Your guidance in every situation.

Thank You that You desire to lead me into the fullness of Your special plan for my life.

(Invite Jesus to guide you. Listen. Perhaps open your Bible **ONCE** if praying about a particular situation.)

"Do You Love Me?"

A third time, Jesus asked, "Simon, son of John, do you love me?" Peter was upset that He asked him the third time, and replied, "Lord, You know all things. You know I love You." Jesus replied, "Feed my sheep." Jn 22:17

In asking Peter the three times, "Do you love Me?" Jesus was putting down a marker:- if we really love Him, then we will seek to feed His sheep.

"Anyone who has discovered Christ must lead others to Him."
Pope Benedict

"Once I have Jesus, I have to bring Him to others."
Blessed Mother Teresa

Lord, grant that I may never miss an opportunity to help another person in their spiritual journey.

May I never be held back by my shyness or lack of courage. Empower me, Lord, with the outpouring of the Holy Spirit.

Put a new courage into my heart. Put the right words on my lips. Inspire me to give the right gifts.

And give me a passion for leading people to You.

(Pause. Mentally picture yourself reaching out to others.)

Heroic Forgiveness

"Forgive us our sins as we forgive everyone who sins against us." Luke 11:4

"When you forgive those who sin against you, it opens you to the forgiving love of your heavenly Father"
Mt 6:14

Praying with the heart and voice of Jesus, requires heroic forgiveness.

This isn't to suggest that God doesn't love you if there is hurt in your life, or that you won't often see your prayers answered.

But if we are to pray with the voice of Jesus, then we need to forgive with the forgiveness of Jesus.

Lord Jesus, in faith, I now decide to forgive completely and totally every person who has ever hurt me or who ever will hurt me, including ......

Help me to take the right steps to come into this level of forgiveness, and the right steps to act out this type of unconditional forgiveness.

(Pause. Unite yourself with the forgiveness of Jesus)

Heroic Thanksgiving

"Even if the whole world is collapsing, I will rejoice in God, and exult in the Lord my Saviour." Hab 3:16-17

"Rejoice in the Lord in every situation. Again I say, Rejoice." Phil 4:4

You don't have to thank God that someone is an alcoholic, but if you desire to pray with the voice of Jesus, then you do need to start thanking God for the person who is the alcoholic - and for God's love.

There are, of course, times for grieving, and times for working through one's emotions, but to see mighty answers to prayer, the spirit of praise and thanksgiving is necessary.

Lord Jesus, thank You that you will bring good for me out of every bad thing that has ever happened to me or ever will happen to me.

Thank You, Lord, that You are with me in every situation; and that in You, there is the answer to every problem.

With Mary I pray, "My soul glorifies the Lord, my spirit rejoices in God my Saviour." (Luke 1:46-47)

(Pause. Let thanksgiving well up within you.)

Praying For Deliverance

"Put on all God's armour, for it isn't just flesh and blood we fight, but a whole host of evil spirits." Eph 6:11-12

"I have given you power to tread underfoot evil spirits and to overcome all the power of the enemy" Lk 10:19.

Evil spirits are like viruses. Wherever one has a weak spot, they will infect. This is a not possession, but it intensifies one's compulsion. One then needs deliverance.

Where there is a severe problem, there will be several different spirits - for example behind the spirit of alcoholism, there may also be the spirits of self-deception, despair, manipulation, anger etc., etc.

When praying, we are not concerned as to where the human spirit ends and the evil spirit enters in. If a person is bitter, we pray for deliverance from the spirit of bitterness, without the need to distinguish between the human spirit of bitterness and the evil spirit which latches on to it.

Grant me, Lord, the grace to break every sin or compulsion that could give any power of evil an entry point into my life.

Lord Jesus, by your mighty power, may my home, my family, and everything I own be protected against all evil.

Enable me, Lord, to pray with power over all the works of the evil one.

(Regularly bless your home etc. with holy water.)

For One Who Rejects God

Lord I forgive ..... completely and totally for every way (s)he has ever hurt me or ever will hurt me.

I thank You that You love .... even if (s)he has turned his (her) back on you.

Pause to become aware of ...... as a real living human being with feelings and emotions.

Become conscious of Jesus' great love for .... and His desire to lead him (her) to a living relationship with Himself.

Then with love in your heart, and pausing after each line, pray,

Lord Jesus, I cry out to You for ......   Help him (her) to come to a living relationship with you.

Deliver him (her) Lord, from the spirit of rebellion, from spiritual darkness, and from all evil spirits.

**Lord, grant .... the grace of a real spiritual breakthrough;
The grace to somehow come to a living relationship with You, and to start walking with You.**

(Pause. Hold ... before Jesus, with longing in your heart.)

For One Who Is Depressed

Lord I forgive ..... completely and totally for every way (s)he has ever hurt me or ever will hurt me.

I thank You that You love ... and that You desire to set him (her) free from depression.

Pause to become aware of ...... as a real living human being with feelings and emotions. Become conscious that for .... life is a real struggle.

Become conscious of Jesus' great love for him (her) and His desire to heal him (her). Unite yourself with this love.

Then with love in your heart, and pausing after each line, pray,

Lord Jesus, I cry out to You for ...... who now finds life so difficult.

Deliver ...... from the spirit of depression, from the spirit of despair, from the spirit of fear and anxiety, from the spirit of insecurity, from the spirit of self-hatred, and from all evil spirits.

**Lord, grant .... the grace to trust You,
The grace to start drawing strength from You,
The grace to know that with Your help, (s)he can get on with the simple things of daily life.**

And the grace to receive the best possible help.

(Pause. Hold ... before Jesus, with longing in your heart.)

For An Alcoholic or Addict

Lord I forgive ..... completely and totally for every way (s)he has ever hurt me or ever will hurt me.

I thank You for ....., including for his (her) personality which challenges us to a strong love.

Pause to become aware of ...... as a real living human being with feelings and emotions.

Become conscious of Jesus' great love for .... and His desire to set ..... free. Unite yourself with this love.

Then with love in your heart, and pausing after each line, pray,

Lord Jesus, I cry out to You for ...... and h.. family.

Deliver ...... Lord, from the spirit of alcoholism.
(**OR** from the spirit of drug addiction).
Deliver him (her) also from the spirit of denial, from the spirit of bitterness, from the spirit of dependency, from the spirit of manipulation and from all evil spirits.

Lord, grant ... the grace to turn to You,
The grace to want to be delivered,
The grace to trust in Your power to set him (her) free,
The grace to seek the help (s)he needs.

(Pause. Hold ... before Jesus, with longing in your heart.)

For One Suffering Anorexia

Lord I forgive ..... completely and totally for every way (s)he has ever hurt me or ever will hurt me.

I thank You that You love .... and desire to heal her (him).

Pause to become aware of ...... as a real living human being, whose inner emotions and feelings may have become knotted or tangled.

Become conscious of Jesus' great love for ....; His desire to permeate her (him) with His love. Unite yourself with this love.

Then with love in your heart, and pausing after each line, pray,

Lord Jesus, I cry out to You for ......

Deliver her (him) Lord from the spirit of anorexia, from the spirit of self hatred, from the spirit of denial, from the spirit of manipulation, and from all evil spirits.

**Fill and permeate her (his) heart with Your love.
Give her (him) the desire to be healed.
Help her (him) to trust You for transformation.
Bring her (his) inner being back to life.**

Come alive within her (him), Lord Jesus.

(Pause. Hold ... before Jesus, with longing in your heart.)

For One Who Is Suicidal

Lord I forgive ..... completely and totally for every way (s)he has ever hurt me or ever will hurt me.

I thank You that You love ...... and desire to embrace him (her) in your love.

Pause to become aware of ...... as a real living human being with feelings and emotions.

Become conscious of Jesus' great love for .... and His desire to heal him (her). Unite yourself with this love.

Then with love in your heart, and pausing after each line, pray

Lord Jesus, I cry out to You for ......

Deliver ..... Lord, from the spirit of suicide, from the spirit of despair, from the spirit of desolation, from the spirit of distrust in You, and from all evil spirits.

Lord, fill .....'s heart with Your love.
Help him (her) trust You for the future.
Bring joy and hope into his (her) life.
Protect him (her) from all evil.

(Pause. Hold .... before Jesus, with longing in your heart.)

For One Who Is Bitter

Lord I forgive ..... completely and totally for every way (s)he has ever hurt me or ever will hurt me.

I thank You that You love ...... and desire to deliver him (her) from bitterness.

Pause to become aware of ...... as a real human being with feelings and emotions, who has perhaps suffered real hurt and disappointments in life.

Become conscious of Jesus' great love for .... and His desire to set him (her) free. Unite yourself with this love.

Then with love in your heart, and pausing after each line, pray

Lord Jesus, I cry out to You for ......

Deliver ..... Lord, from the spirit of bitterness, from the spirit of revenge, from the spirit of hatred and from all evil spirits.

Lord, draw ..... into an experience of Your love. Help him (her) to let go of the hurts he (she) now feels, to forgive and to take the steps that lead to healing.

Help him (her) to surrender everything to You and to trust You.

(Pause. Hold .... before Jesus, with longing in your heart.)

For One Who Is Separated

Lord I forgive ..... completely and totally for any way (s)he has ever hurt me or ever will hurt me.

I thank you for ......, and that You desire to fill the great gap that is now in his (her) life.

Pause to become aware of ...... as a real living human being with feelings and emotions, who may now be hurting deeply.

Become conscious of Jesus' great love for ..... Unite yourself with this love.

Then, with love in your heart and pausing after each line, pray,

Lord Jesus, I cry out to You for .... Grant him (her) the grace to surrender his (her) life to You, and to trust You for the future.
Lord, heal all ....'s emotional wounds.

Deliver ..... Lord, from the spirit of hurt, the spirit of bitterness, the spirit of embarrassment, and from all evil spirits.

Lord, draw ..... into Your loving embrace.
Protect him (her) from all harm. Fill him (her) with Your strength.

(Pause. Hold .... before Jesus, with longing in your heart)

Protection On The Roads

"As we travelled the road to Jerusalem, the hand of the Lord protected us from accidents, bandits, and from dangerous fellow travellers." Ezra 8:31

Living in Jesus has major implications for how one drives.

Here too we are called to be His hands, His heart, His mind, His eyes, His ears and His feet.

We also need God's protection because some drivers leave themselves open to being used by evil spirits, while evil spirits can sometimes take advantage of any defect in road or car or a moment's distraction by the driver.

Lord, teach me how to be Your hands, Your feet, Your eyes, Your heart and Your mind when driving.

Deliver me from any spirit that could affect my driving, especially the spirit of ..... (and the spirit of ...)

I entrust my car to You. Send Your angels to watch over it. Protect us on the roads from all serious accidents and from all evil.

(Mentally picture yourself being Jesus' hands when driving.)

To offer this prayer for someone else just replace "me" with that person's name, etc.

For This Day, Lord

"It is no longer I who live, but Christ who lives in me. This union with Jesus, I live by ongoing faith" Gal 2:20.

"We are being transformed from one degree of likeness to Jesus to another." 2 Cor 3:18

You are called to become the living presence of Jesus, to become His hands and His voice in today's world.

Don't be frightened. Just relax into Jesus who is within you.

With total trust in Jesus, ask His help to enable you to stand in His place moment by moment for this day.

**Lord for this day,
May my heart be Your heart,
May my thoughts be Your thoughts,
May my hands be Your hands,
May my feet be Your feet,
May my eyes be Your eyes,
May my ears be Your ears,
May my voice be Your voice,
And may my face be Your face.**

(Pause. Relax. Allow the presence of Jesus within you to flow through you.)